Follow Me Around™
Ireland

By Wiley Blevins

SCHOLASTIC

Content Consultant: Caleb Richardson, PhD, Assistant Professor, Department of History, University of New Mexico, Albuquerque, New Mexico

Library of Congress Cataloging-in-Publication Data
Names: Blevins, Wiley, author.
Title: Ireland / by Wiley Blevins.
Description: New York, NY : Children's Press, an imprint of Scholastic Inc.,
2018. | Series: Follow me around | Includes bibliographical references and index.
Identifiers: LCCN 2017038395 | ISBN 9780531234600 (library binding) | ISBN 9780531243725 (pbk.)
Subjects: LCSH: Ireland—Juvenile literature.
Classification: LCC DA906 .B59 2018 | DDC 941.7—dc23
LC record available at https://lccn.loc.gov/2017038395

Design: Judith Christ Lafond & Anna Tunick Tabachnik
Text: Wiley Blevins
© 2018 Scholastic Inc.

All rights reserved. Published in 2018 by Children's Press, an imprint of Scholastic Inc.
Printed in North Mankato, MN, USA 113
SCHOLASTIC, CHILDREN'S PRESS, and associated logos are trademarks and/or registered trademarks of Scholastic Inc.
Scholastic Inc., 557 Broadway, New York, NY 10012

1 2 3 4 5 6 7 8 9 10 R 27 26 25 24 23 22 21 20 19 18

Photos ©: cover background: espiegle/iStockphoto; cover boy: Nick Daly/age fotostock; 0 back cover: Nick Daly/age fotostock; 1: Nick Daly/age fotostock; 3: VeraPetruk/iStockphoto; 4 left: Nick Daly/age fotostock; 6 left: Macsnap/iStockphoto; 6 right: Chris Hill/Getty Images; 7 left: Spencer Grant/Getty Images; 7 right: pniesen/iStockphoto; 8 top left: grandriver/iStockphoto; 8 top right: Oliver Strewe/Getty Images; 8 center: Simon Reddy/Alamy Images; 8 bottom: AS Food studio/Shutterstock; 9 top left: mtreasure/iStockphoto; 9 top right: foodandwinephotography/iStockphoto; 9 center: Brent Hofacker/Shutterstock; 9 bottom: Richard Jung/Getty Images; 10 left: Winfield Parks/National Geographic/Getty Images; 10 right: Dag Sundberg/Getty Images; 11: Stephanie Maze/Getty Images; 12 top: Nikiteev_Konstantin/iStockphoto; 12 bottom: Kerdkanno/Shutterstock; 12 -13 background: Vadim Yerofeyev/Dreamstime; 13 center: lynea/Shutterstock; 13 top left: GlobalP/iStockphoto; 13 top right: GlobalP/iStockphoto; 13 bottom: Libor Dušek/Dreamstime; 14 top left: sasar/iStockphoto; 14 top right: David Soanes Photography/Getty Images; 14 bottom: Victor Maschek/Shutterstock; 15 left: Leonid Andronov/iStockphoto; 15 top right: Universal Images Group North America LLC/DeAgostini/Alamy Images; 15 bottom right: Franck Seguin/Corbis/VCG/Getty Images; 16 left: Ken Welsh/Getty Images; 16 top right: George Munday/Design Pics/Getty Images; 16 bottom right: Christophe Boisvieux/age fotostock; 17 left: Les Gibbon/Alamy Images; 17 right: mbbirdy/iStockphoto; 18 top: Popperfoto/Getty Images; 18 bottom left: Hulton-Deutsch Collection/Corbis/Getty Images; 18 bottom right: National Geographic Stock: Vintage Collection/The Granger Collection; 19 left: Henry Guttmann/Getty Images; 19 right: aaabbbccc/Shutterstock; 20 right: Kerdkanno/Shutterstock; 20 left: VeraPetruk/iStockphoto; 21 top: Alan Becker/Getty Images; 21 bottom: Niall Carson - PA Images/Getty Images; 22 left: JoeFoxBelfast/Radharc Images/Alamy Images; 22 right: North Wind Picture Archives/Alamy Images; 23 top left: Peter Mukly/Alamy Images; 23 center left: Julien Behal - PA Images/Getty Images; 23 bottom left: George Sweeney/Alamy Images; 23 right: rudvi/Shutterstock; 24 left: Design Pics Inc/Getty Images; 24 right, 25 left: Clodagh Kilcoyne/Getty Images; 25 center: Design Pics Inc/Alamy Images; 25 right: Stephen Barnes/Alamy Images; 26 top: O'Dea/Wikimedia; 26 center: levers2007/iStockphoto; 26 bottom: Londonpicscapital/Dreamstime; 27 left: Hulton Archive/Getty Images; 27 right: Design Pics Inc/Getty Images; 28 A: DEA/S. VANNINI/Getty Images; 28 B: Tim Graham/Getty Images; 28 C: DEA/S. VANNINI/Getty Images; 28 D: IIC/Axiom/Getty Images; 28 E: DEA/S. VANNINI/Getty Images; 28 F: Michael Diggin/Alamy Images; 30 top right: ASUWAN MASAE/Shutterstock; 30 top left: Leontura/iStockphoto; 30 bottom: Nick Daly/age fotostock.

Maps by Jim McMahon.

Table of Contents

USA

Ireland

Where in the World Is Ireland?

Dia dhuit (JEE-ah GHWITCH), or hello, from Ireland! I'm Seamus (SHAY-mus), your tour guide. My name is the Irish word for "James." Irish, or Gaelic, is one of the languages we speak in Ireland. The other main language is English.

Ireland is on an island in northwestern Europe. Our grassy fields are so bright green that the island is nicknamed the Emerald Isle. The island is divided in two. My country, the Republic of Ireland, takes up most of the island. Northern Ireland is on the northeastern section. It is a part of the United Kingdom.

The Republic of Ireland, which we often just call Ireland, offers many things to see and do. As we say, *céad míle fáilte* (KAY-ehd MEE-leh FAHYLE-chuh)—a hundred thousand welcomes!

Fast Facts:

- Ireland covers 27,133 square miles (70,274 square kilometers).

- Wherever you are in Ireland, you are no more than 70 miles (113 km) from the sea.

- The island's landscape is shaped like a bowl. Flat plains are at the center, surrounded by mountains on the coastline.

- Ireland's coasts touch several bodies of water—the Atlantic Ocean, Celtic Sea, Irish Sea, and St. George's Channel.

- The climate is mild—not too hot in summer and rarely below freezing in winter. But it can still be chilly when it rains—and it rains a lot!

- The 240-mile-long (386 km) River Shannon is Ireland's longest river.

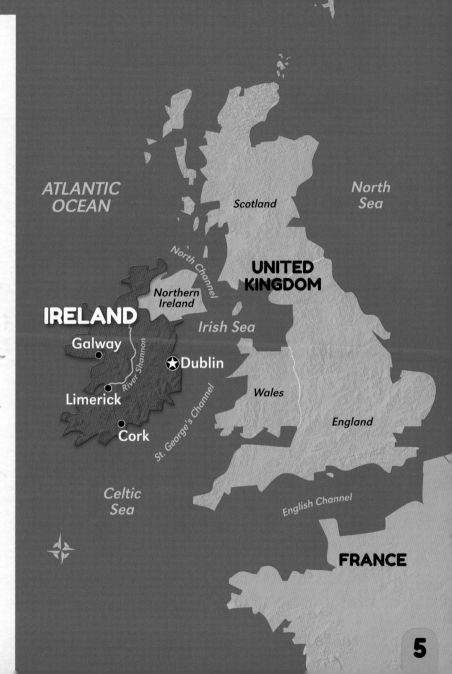

ATLANTIC OCEAN

North Sea

Scotland

North Channel

UNITED KINGDOM

Northern Ireland

IRELAND

Irish Sea

Galway

River Shannon

Dublin

Limerick

Wales

St. George's Channel

England

Cork

Celtic Sea

English Channel

FRANCE

Many homes and businesses line the River Liffey in Dublin.

Pub

Home Sweet Home

I am from Dublin, Ireland. I live with my parents and little sister above a pub that my parents run. Pubs are popular meeting places in Ireland. There are hundreds in my city! Kids are allowed in pubs for a meal until 9 p.m. After that, it's adults only. You'll hear a lot of traditional Irish music in our pub.

While I live in the city, about 42 percent of Irish people live in the country, including my uncle and cousins. I love to visit them! Like many country residents, they live in a cottage. Irish cottages are small homes made from local stone. They have roofs made of thatch, such as straw, or slate, a type of flat rock. They also have thick walls and small windows to keep the heat in. That's really important because it can be very chilly in my rainy country!

Many people paint their cottages with whitewash, which is made of water and white powder.

Chatting

We Irish are known for being very friendly and easygoing. Don't be surprised if you get a good slagging. That's teasing! Slagging shows we like you and feel comfortable around you. And don't be afraid to slag back.

Many Irish also love to chat. Anywhere. Anytime. About anything. If you can't think of something to chat about, start with the weather. There's always something to talk about when it comes to our quick-changing skies. While chatting with the locals, you will probably be asked, "Are you on holiday?" That means, "Are you on vacation?" That question is often followed by a list of fun things to do. We want to make sure our visitors have a great time exploring our country.

Boxty

Corned beef

Cabbage

Dinner is often served with a main dish of roasted meat.

Let's Eat

When it comes to food in Ireland, it's all about the potato. We have many yummy potato dishes. One of my favorites is *boxty*. It's a potato pancake made with grated potato, flour, and egg. You can add some sugar or cream on top to make a special treat called a *stampy*. Another potato dish is *colcannon*. It's mashed

Boxty

Colcannon

potatoes mixed with kale or cabbage. As part of a tradition, the cook sometimes hides a ring or coin inside the colcannon. Each person at the table scoops out a big spoonful. The person who finds the ring is said to be the next to marry. The person who finds the coin is said to become rich someday. I always hope for the coin!

A meal of fish and chips is sometimes called a one and one.

Carrageen pudding

You'll get soda bread with almost any Irish meal. It's hard and crusty on the outside but soft on the inside. You should also try our thick Irish stew. It's usually made with mutton (from sheep), potatoes, onions, carrots, and sometimes turnips.

Because we're surrounded by lots of water, we eat our fair share of seafood. Small restaurants called chippers are the best places to grab my favorite meal from the sea: fish and chips. Chips are what you call fries. It is worth standing in the long **queue** that often forms at the best chippers.

Want something sweet? Try carrageen moss pudding. Despite its name, this pudding is made from red seaweed, not moss. I love it! There's also a tasty chocolate version.

Soda bread

Irish stew

9

My friends are always very focused during the lessons.

School lunch

Off to School

In Ireland, we go to school until at least the age of 16. Many students go on to college because it's free here. That's right. No cost!

One of the first things we learn in school is how to read and write English. We also learn Irish. Everyone here spoke Irish until the 1800s. Now, more people speak English than Irish. About 41 percent, however, speak at least some Irish. And roughly 6 percent of kids attend a *gaelscoil*. All the classes there are taught in Irish.

Irish words don't use the letters *j, k, q, w, x, y*, or *z*. Most of the consonants we do use can be pronounced in more than one way, depending on what letter comes after it. Also, vowels can have an accent mark, called a *fada*. It makes the vowel sound longer. For example, *te* (TEH) means "hot or warm," and *té* (TAY) means "person."

cara
(KAH-ruh)
friend

Gaelscoil

Counting to 10 in Irish

Knowing how to count to 10 in Irish is helpful, particularly in areas where Irish is widely spoken.

1	a haon *(ah HAYN)*
2	a dó *(ah DOH)*
3	a trí *(ah TREE)*
4	a ceathair *(ah KAH-her)*
5	a cúig *(ah KOO-ig)*
6	a sé *(ah SHAY)*
7	a seacht *(ah SHAHKT)*
8	a hocht *(ah HUKT)*
9	a naoi *(ah NAY)*
10	a deich *(ah DEH)*

Want to learn some Irish slang? Here are a few useful words.

Irish Slang	English
bog *(BAHG)*	toilet
craic *(KRAK)*	fun time
gank *(GANGK)*	disgusting
piped telly *(PIPET TEHL-ee)*	cable TV

Limericks!

In Ireland, we have special poems called limericks. That word might sound familiar. It's the name of one of our largest cities and the name of one of our 26 counties. These poems are usually funny. They always have five lines. Lines 1, 2, and 5 rhyme with one another. They usually have eight or nine beats, or syllables. Lines 3 and 4 have five or six beats and rhyme with each other.

Here are a few limericks for you to enjoy. One was written by the famous author Edward Lear. Try writing a limerick about someone or someplace you know well.

There was an old man of Peru
Who dreamt he was eating his shoe.
He awoke in the night,
With a terrible fright,
And found it was perfectly true.

There once was a shamrock named Pat,
Who tripped on a root and went splat,
She ripped her best leaf,
And sobbed in her grief,
And ruined her favorite hat.

There was an old man of Dumbree,
Who taught little owls to drink tea;
For he said, "To eat mice,
Is not proper or nice,"
So my friends you must let them go free.

There was an Old Man in a boat,
Who said, "I'm afloat, I'm afloat!"
When they said, "No! you ain't!"
He was ready to faint,
That unhappy Old Man in a boat.
—by Edward Lear

An elderly man called Keith
Mislaid his set of false teeth –
They'd been laid on a chair,
He'd forgot they were there,
Sat down, and was bitten beneath.

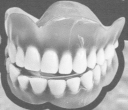

13

Phoenix Park

Dublin Spire

Touring Ireland

Dublin: Capital City

Welcome to my city, Dublin. It's the capital of Ireland and almost 10 times bigger than any other city in the country. When you visit, you'll want to go first to the Dublin Spire. At 398 feet (121 meters), it's the city's tallest structure. When the sunlight hits this steel **monument**, it looks like it's changing colors. Wow!

Throne in Dublin Castle

The spire is so tall that you can see it for miles.

Next, head over to Dublin Castle. King John of England built it in 1204. Visit the Throne Room and you'll feel like royalty. After that, explore Phoenix Park. This park is completely surrounded by an old wall. Inside you'll spot the home of Ireland's president.

Bridge over the River Liffey

The interior of a medieval house at Dublinia

DART

You'll see a lot of bridges in my city. They crisscross the River Liffey. If you want a break, go to my favorite spot: the AquaZone at the National Aquatic Centre. It has a wave pool, waterslides, a surfing machine, and more. Get wet and have fun!

One last thing you must see is Dublinia in the Old City. You will learn about **medieval** Dublin when the Vikings lived here. You can even attend a medieval fair. Try on clothing or visit the pie stall. Check out the medicine tent for a look at how doctors worked long ago (if you're not too squeamish!). You can also play an old-style drum or learn to juggle. So much to do!

To dart off to nearby cities and villages for a quieter experience, take the DART. That's the Dublin Area Rapid Transit. This train is fast and affordable.

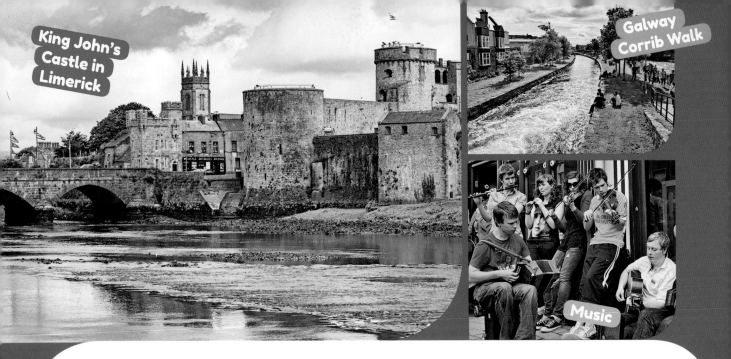

King John's Castle in Limerick

Galway Corrib Walk

Music

Other Big Cities

Speaking of Vikings, go to Limerick. This city started as a Viking settlement in about 812. It lies on the River Shannon, Ireland's longest river. Two must-see sights are King John's Castle and a church called St. Mary's Cathedral. Both buildings are more than 800 years old!

Next, head to Galway. This city is chock-full of medieval buildings. You're sure to hear traditional Irish music here, from a lively dancing jig to a beautiful solo song called *sean-nós* (SHAWN-nohs). This is also one place where you can use your new Irish vocabulary!

Lastly, weave south along our winding roads to Cork on the coast. You can hop on a boat to tour the nearby smaller islands. You might even spot a circus, or group, of puffins!

Bog

Cliffs of Moher

Other Fun Places

Take time to stop at one of the castles that dot the Irish countryside. My favorite is the Rock of Cashel. It is a small hill with an ancient castle sitting on top. Other popular castles include Blarney Castle and Ashford Castle, which is now a luxury hotel.

Don't forget to stop at one of our six national parks. We visit Connemara National Park every summer. It has mountains, lakes, **bogs**, and a lot of animals and rare plants.

Head west to the Atlantic Ocean to see the famous Cliffs of Moher. It's the most visited natural landmark in Ireland—and for good reason! Stand at the top of these cliffs for a view of the ragged, beautiful coastline and the ocean far below.

Our Fascinating History

We're proud of our country's long history. More than 2,500 years ago, the Celts divided the land into small territories. Each had its own ruler, or king. The rulers took advice from the Druids, highly educated teachers and priests.

St. Patrick

Then came the Vikings from Scandinavia. They established many settlements that grew into our biggest cities. Soon after, the English invaded and stayed for centuries.

Timeline: Ireland's History

6,000 BCE

Early tribes
Ireland's earliest inhabitants were probably hunters from Scotland.

600 BCE

Celts (Druids)
Celtic tribes from Europe invade the island to farm and raise cattle. They still influence today's Irish culture.

400s CE

The Golden Age
According to a legend, an Englishman named Patrick drives the "snakes" (Druids) out of Ireland.

800

Vikings
Vikings from Norway invade. They start settlements at Limerick, Cork, and other places.

18

By the late 1800s, we in Ireland wanted more say in how we ruled ourselves. However, our country was divided. Nationalists wanted to separate from the United Kingdom and form their own nation. Unionists wanted to stay with the United Kingdom. The two groups fought bitterly. Finally, in 1922 the Nationalists formed the Republic of Ireland (my country). The Unionists in the north remained a part of the United Kingdom. That land became Northern Ireland.

Emigrants leaving Ireland

mid-1100s

English
The English invade and begin a rule that will last for 750 years.

1845–1849

Potato famine
Irish potato crops fail. More than one million Irish die. Millions more sail to the United States.

1922–1948

Irish Free State/Éire
The Irish govern themselves but are still part of the British Empire.

1948

Republic of Ireland
Ireland becomes a republic and breaks all ties with the United Kingdom.

It Came From Ireland

When people think of Ireland, they often think of the shamrock. It's a three-leaf clover. Saint Patrick, our **patron saint**, used it in his religious teachings. Although it's not an official symbol of my country, you'll see shamrocks everywhere. And if you happen to find a rare four-leaf clover, bravo! We consider it a symbol of good luck.

Leprechauns can also bring good luck. Leprechauns are a type of fairy common to Irish folklore. According to the stories, they look like tiny old men dressed in green or red coats. They make trouble, so be careful. Legend has it that if you catch one, it will lead you to a pot of gold. But don't look away, or the fairy and the gold will vanish!

No trip to Ireland is complete until you've kissed the Blarney Stone. This stone is in the wall of Blarney Castle near Cork, Ireland. Legend has it that anyone who kisses the stone gets the "gift of gab." He or she can flatter people into doing anything! But kissing the stone isn't easy. You have to climb to the castle's peak and then lean over backward to reach the stone.

Wet, soft areas of land called bogs cover about one-sixth of my country. Bogs are special places. Recently, bodies of ancient people have been found in them. These "bog people" are very well preserved. We can learn a lot from them about how people lived long ago.

Druid ceremony

Stingy Jack

Celebrate!

Everyone loves a holiday, and we have some fun ones in Ireland. Halloween is my favorite. It began in Ireland! Long ago, this celebration was called *Samhain* (SAU-een). It occurred on October 31, the night before the Celtic New Year. The Celts believed the spirits of the dead returned that night. Ancient Druid priests collected nuts, apples, and eggs from each home during Samhain.

If a household gave no treats, the Druids played tricks on them. Some say that Celts dressed in costumes to scare away evil spirits, too. This became today's tradition of trick-or-treating. Also, many local Irish people hollowed out turnips and carved faces on them. Some put a candle inside. They called the turnips Stingy Jack or Jack O'Lantern. Does this all sound familiar? It should!

St. Patrick's Day (The Feast of St. Patrick)

March

We celebrate the patron saint of Ireland with parades, fireworks, and Irish language lessons. Many people wear green, a color that represents Ireland. This holiday is also big in the United States!

Puck Fair

August

Go to county Kerry for this unique two-day festival where a wild goat is crowned king.

Christmas

December

This is Ireland's biggest holiday. We attend church, decorate trees, and see traditional plays performed by special actors called mummers (pictured left). We also place holly and ivy wreaths on the graves of loved ones.

Make a Celtic Design

Supplies: potato putty (see recipe below), rolling pin, waxed paper, knife, paper, pencil, paintbrush, sandpaper

Potato Putty Recipe: Dissolve ½ cup dried potato flakes in ½ cup warm water. Mix in ¼ cup white glue, 1 tablespoon green acrylic paint, 1 cup cornstarch, and 1 cup flour.

Directions:

Ask an adult to help!

1 **Roll** the putty between two sheets of waxed paper until it's about ⅛ inch thick. **Cut** out a square the size you want.

2 **Copy** the design above on a piece of paper. Place your design on the square. **Trace over** the design with the end of the paintbrush handle to form indents in the putty.

3 **Remove** the design. Use the paintbrush to **push down** the putty around the design so the design appears raised.

4 Allow the putty to dry. Then **sand** it with the sandpaper.

Gaelic football

Time to Play

Kids in Ireland love their sports. The faster the better! Gaelic football, hurling, and horseback riding are really popular. Hurling is similar to lacrosse and field hockey. It is a fast-paced ball game. We use an ax-shaped stick called a *hurley* to play. The team that gets the small ball across the goal the most times wins. But this sport can be a bit rough. Expect to walk away with a few bruises and scrapes!

Gaelic football is an ancient Celtic game. It's similar to soccer and rugby. This sport is unique to our country, and it has been popular for centuries. But like hurling, this game is rough. Bruises and scrapes are common here, too!

Laytown Races

Hurling

Irish step dance

We love our horses in Ireland. You can watch flat races, which are on flat ground and often cover long distances. Races called steeplechases involve **hurdles** such as fences and ditches. One of the most famous races, the Laytown Races, is held on the beach. It is a must-see!

Dancing is another much-loved activity in Ireland. My sister and I, like many Irish kids, study step dancing in school. We learn the traditional Celtic style *sean nós*. When we perform, we wear special outfits with Celtic designs. And nothing sounds better than some great Irish music. The instruments we use include the Irish harp, bagpipes called *uilleann* (IHL-uhn) pipes, fiddles, tin whistles, and the *bodhrán* (BOWR-ahn). That's the Irish drum, which many people call the "heartbeat" of our music.

You Won't Believe This!

We have some long place names in Ireland. One of the longest has 22 letters! It's a town called *Muckanaghederdauhaulia*. The name means "pig marsh between two seas." Now that's a mouthful to say!

Ireland is perfect for raising animals such as horses, cattle, and sheep. In fact, you'll find more cattle and sheep than people in Ireland!

Do you like to read about world records? Who is the fastest human being? The tallest man? The most socks ever worn on one foot? (It's 152!) You can find fascinating facts like these in *Guinness World Records*. The book started right here in Ireland in 1955!

Ever heard of a fairy fort? Believe it or not, they are real! They are the **ruins** of ancient *crannogs*. These round buildings were built thousands of years ago on small, human-made islands in the middle of lakes. Crannogs were difficult for invaders to reach, and the buildings could withstand bow and arrow attacks. Only a few fairy forts remain today.

Crannog reconstruction at Connamara Heritage and History Centre

If you like books, you'll find one of the oldest and most beautiful at Trinity College in Dublin. *The Book of Kells* is a Bible created in about 800 CE. The pages are decorated with elaborate designs and colorful illustrations of people and animals!

Guessing Game!

Here are some other great sites around Ireland. If you have time, try to see them all!

Marvel at the beautiful natural formations in these rocky caves.

F

1. Skellig Rocks
2. **The Burren**
3. St. Patrick's Cathedral
4. Crag Cave
5. Clare Island
6. Newgrange Tomb

Built around 3200 BCE and older than the pyramids of Egypt, this tomb has walls lined with gold.

A

Built in 1220, this Dublin cathedral is one of the most famous churches in the world.

E

Drive through county Clare to see the vast area of flat limestone dotted with colorful flowers in late spring and summer.

B

Go to this island to see the ruins of the castle that was home to the famed pirate queen Grace O'Malley.

D

Take a boat ride to the craggy rocks that rise up from the sea miles away from the mainland.

C

A6, B2, C1, D5, E3, F4

Answer Key

Preparing for Your Visit

By now, you should be ready to hop on a plane to Ireland. Here are some tips to prepare for your trip.

1 Before you come to Ireland, exchange your money. Like many other countries in the European Union, we use the *euro*. Take a peek at our coins. You'll see a harp, the symbol of Ireland. You'll need plenty of euros to buy fun **souvenirs**, such as singing leprechauns and **tweed** hats.

2 Bring an umbrella or a raincoat when you visit. Some parts of my country get more than 220 days of rain each year. Also, the weather can change very quickly. One minute it might be sunny, and a short time later it will rain. This happens even in the summer.

3 If you're feeling adventurous, take a bicycle tour. Our quiet roads are ideal for these trips. You can rent a bike in one town and drop it off in another when you become tired. You'll love the fresh air and beautiful scenery as you ride through our narrow and winding roads.

4 There are some useful words to know as you travel. *Fir* (FIHR) means "men" and *mná* (MNAW) means "women." Look for these words if you need a restroom. Speaking of restroom, the word for "toilet" is *leithreas* (LEH-hrihs). And if you need help, just call the *gardaí* (GAHR-dee), or "police." *Dúnta* (DOON-tuh) means "closed," and *oscailte* (OS-kel-teh) means "open."

29

The United States Compared to Ireland

Official Name	United States of America (USA)	The Republic of Ireland
Official Language	No official language, though English is most commonly used	Irish and English
Population	325 million	More than 4.5 million
Common Words	yes, no, please, thank you	*tá or sea, níl or ní hea, le do thoil, go raibh maith agat*
Flag		
Money	Dollar	Euro
Location	North America	Northern Europe
Highest Point	Denali (Mount McKinley)	Carrauntoohil, county Kerry
Lowest Point	Death Valley	North Slob, county Wexford
Size	World's third-largest country	Slightly larger than West Virginia
National Anthem	"The Star-Spangled Banner"	"Amhrán na bhFiann"

So now you know some important and fascinating things about my country, Ireland. I hope to see you someday trekking through our countryside villages, munching on a plate of fish and chips at my parents' pub, or exploring one of our medieval towns. Until then . . . *slán*. Good-bye!

Glossary

bogs
(BAHGZ)
areas of soft, wet land

hurdles
(HUR-duhlz)
small barriers, such as fences, that you jump over in a race

medieval
(mee-DEE-vuhl)
of or having to do with the Middle Ages, a period of history from about 1000 to 1450

monument
(MAHN-yuh-muhnt)
a statue, building, or other structure that reminds people of an event or person

patron saint
(PAY-truhn SAYNT)
a saint, or holy person, who is believed to look after an individual, a group of people, a particular activity, a city, or a country

queue
(KYOO)
a line of people who are waiting for something

ruins
(ROO-inz)
the remains of something that has collapsed or been destroyed

souvenirs
(soo-vuh-NEERZ)
objects that are kept to remind you of a place, a person, or something that happened

tweed
(TWEED)
a rough wool cloth woven with yarns of two or more colors

Index

Facts for Now

Visit this Scholastic website for more information on Ireland and to download the Teaching Guide for this series:

www.factsfornow.scholastic.com   Enter the keyword **Ireland**

About the Author

Wiley Blevins is an author living and working in New York City. His greatest love is traveling, and he has been all over the  world. He has written several books for children, including the Ick and Crud series and the Scary Tales Retold series.